HOW

You Can Study the Bible Effectively

BILL BRIGHT

NewLife
PUBLICATIONS

P.O. Box 593684
Orlando, FL 32859-3684

How You Can Study the Bible Effectively

Published by
NewLife Publications
A ministry of Campus Crusade for Christ
P.O. Box 620877
Orlando, FL 32862-0877

Edited by Joette Whims.

Design and production by Genesis Group.

Printed in the United States of America.

NewLife2000 is a registered service mark of Campus Crusade for Christ.

ISBN 1-56399-127-6

Contents of this book have been adapted from the *Ten Basic Steps Toward
Christian Maturity* and other *NewLife* Publications products.

Unless otherwise indicated, Scripture quotations are from the *New Living
Translation*, © 1996 by Tyndale Charitable Trust.

Unless otherwise indicated, Scripture quotations are taken from the *New International Version*, © 1973, 1978, 1984 by the International Bible Society. Published by Zondervan Bible Publishers, Grand Rapids, Michigan.

Scripture quotations designated TLB are from *The Living Bible*, © 1971 by
Tyndale House Publishers, Wheaton, Illinois.

As a personal policy, Bill Bright has never accepted honorariums
or royalties for his personal use. Any royalties from this book are
dedicated to the glory of God and designated to the various min-
istries of Campus Crusade for Christ/*NewLife2000*.

What Is a Transferable Concept?

*W*hen our Lord commanded the eleven men with whom He had most shared His earthly ministry to go into all the world and make disciples of all nations, He told them to teach these new disciples all that He had taught them (Matthew 28:18–20).

Later the apostle Paul gave the same instructions to Timothy: "The things you have heard me say in the presence of many witnesses entrust to reliable men who will also be qualified to teach others" (2 Timothy 2:2, NIV).

According to many reliable surveys and polls approximately 50 percent of church members are not sure of their salvation. Approximately 95 percent of church members do not understand the person and ministry of the Holy Spirit, and as a result live defeated, frustrated, fruitless lives. And 98 percent of professing believers do not regularly share their faith in Christ with others.

In our endeavor to help meet these basic needs and to build Christian disciples, Campus Crusade for Christ has developed a series of "how to's"—or "transferable concepts"—in which we discuss many of the basic truths that Jesus and His disciples taught.

A "transferable concept" is an idea or a truth that can be transferred or communicated from one person to another and then to another, spiritual generation after generation, without distorting or diluting its original meaning.

As these basic truths—"transferable concepts"—of the Christian life are made available through the printed word, films, videotapes, and audiocassettes in every major language of the world, they could well be used by God to help transform the lives of tens of millions throughout the world.

We encourage you to master each of these concepts by reading it thoughtfully at least six times[1] until you are personally prepared to communicate it to others "who will also be qualified to teach others." By mastering these basic materials and discipling others to do the same, many millions of men and women are being reached and discipled for Christ and thus are making a dramatic contribution toward the fulfillment of the Great Commission in our generations. I pray that you will be a mighty instrument in God's hands to help fulfill the Great Commission in your generation.

Bill Bright

---

[1] Educational research confirms that the average person can master the content of a concept, such as this one, by reading it thoughtfully six times.

Contents

How You Can Study the Bible Effectively

Staking Our Lives on the Word of God

*C*an you imagine living alone in darkness for six months? During his first Antarctic expedition, Admiral Byrd flew to the South Pole all by himself. He built a small hut to shelter himself from the brutal six-month-long winter night. Blasts of arctic wind and biting, blowing snow buried his small hut every night.

Each day, Admiral Byrd shoveled his way to the surface of the snow. When he broke through, the light was so dim he could see only a dozen yards. If he left his hut, he used the stovepipe sticking out of the snow as a reference point to find his way back.

One day when he turned to go back, he could not see the stovepipe! Although panic threatened to overwhelm him, he refused to move. He knew the danger. If he wandered about looking for his hut, he would probably get further and further away.

Instead, he drove a stake into the snow. Using it as a center, he paced around a large circle looking for the entrance to his hut. He kept one eye on the stake and searched through the darkness with the other. Not finding the hut, he extended his radius and made a bigger circle.

The third time he tried, his circle was so large, he almost lost sight of his stake. He returned and resolved to make one more attempt with an even larger circle.

As he made that fourth round, he strained his eyes to their limit to peer through the darkness. He knew if he lost sight of the stake—his reference point—he would quickly succumb to the ice and snow.

But the fourth time, he walked right into the hut's tunnel.

Do you ever feel like you are wandering through darkness in your life? All of us feel that way at times. Circumstances can overwhelm us. Ailing parents, loss of a job, high mortgages, too many bills, family crises, sickness, and other problems can make us wonder how we will ever find our way.

The world tells us that we have no reference point to help us solve our difficulties. Definite standards and rules are obsolete and intolerable. The future is unknowable and unchangeable, so we should live it up now.

But as Christians, we do have a reference point—the Bible. When we stake our lives on its teachings and principles, God gives us guidance on how to live. When we love, trust, and obey Him and His Word, we will enjoy the abundant life He has promised every believer.

What is there about the Bible that has given it such power to influence and enrich the lives of many millions of believers throughout the centuries around the world? Psalm 119:91 records, "Your laws remain true today, for everything serves your plans." Verse 138 says, "Your decrees are perfect; they are entirely worthy of our trust." The writer of Hebrews emphasizes how the Bible works in our lives, "The word of God is full of living power. It is sharper than the sharpest knife, cutting deep into our innermost thoughts and desires. It exposes us for what we really are" (Hebrews 4:12).

By studying and applying God's Word, we will see our world and ourselves through God's eyes. We will be transformed by the renewing of our minds (Romans 12:2). We will get to know the author, the living God.

In these pages, I will share with you why it is so vital for us to read and study God's Word on a consistent basis. We will discuss how its principles work in the lives of believers and discover practical ways we can study the Bible effectively to apply what we have learned.

The Bible Is a Personal Word from God

*T*he Bible has had a greater influence on this world than any other book. Eighteenth century German philosopher Immanuel Kant said, "The existence of the Bible, as a book for people, is the greatest benefit which the human race has ever experienced." President Herbert Hoover emphasized, "The whole inspiration of our civilization springs from the teachings of Christ and the lessons of the prophets. To read the Bible for these fundamentals is a necessity of American life."[2]

Men and women by the millions, famous and unknown, have changed history because God used the Bible to change them. St. Augustine, Martin Luther, John Calvin, John Wesley, and many others depended on the Scripture to guide their lives, which in turn gave them power to influence the world in which they lived. Daniel Webster, politician and diplomat and one of our country's greatest orators, said of the Bible, "I have read the Bible through many times, and now make it a practice to read it through once every year… It fits man for life—it prepares him for death."[3]

Without some biblical teaching, no one could become a child of God. James writes, "In His goodnsss [God] chose to make us His own children by giving us His true word" (James 1:18). Think back to the day that you first received the simple message of God's love and forgiveness. Which passages

---

[2] William J. Federer, *America's God and Country: Encyclopedia of Quotations* (Coppell, TX: Fame Publishing, Inc., 1994), p. 297.

[3] Ibid., 672.

did God use to reveal Himself to you? Now consider how God has used His Word to influence your life since then. Psalm 19:7,8 says, "The law of the Lord is perfect, reviving the soul. The decrees of the Lord are trustworthy, making wise the simple. The commandments of the Lord are right, bringing joy to the heart. The commands of the Lord are clear, giving insight to life."

I would like to share with you several other reasons why the Bible is the most important book ever written and why it is so urgently important for us to read, study, memorize, and meditate on its truths.

The Bible gives us moral moorings for our lives.

Many years ago while I was a student at Fuller Theological Seminary, two gifted young evangelists spoke at our chapel program. Both believed and preached that the Bible was inspired in every word. Some time later, one of those men rejected the authority and integrity of God's Word. As a result, he lost his moral standard on which to base his life and ministry. He divorced his wife, left the ministry, and eventually became an outspoken antagonist of the Christian faith.

The other young evangelist continued to believe that the Bible is God's Word and is without error. When he could not understand something in the Bible, he trusted that what God said was true. God honored his faith. That man is Billy Graham. God has used him to touch the lives of many millions of people around the world.

The first evangelist's pride of intellect caused him to stand in judgment of God's Word instead of inviting God's Word to judge and guide him. When he ceased to believe that the Bible is God's Word, he was cast adrift on a stormy sea, tossed back and forth by every wind of teaching. The examples of these two men illustrate the saying, "Either God's Word will keep you from sin or sin will keep you from God's Word."

In a letter to Timothy, his beloved son in Christ, Paul wrote, "The whole Bible was given to us by inspiration from God and is useful to teach us what is true and to make us realize what is wrong in our lives; it straightens us out and helps us do what is right. It is God's way of making us well prepared at every point, fully equipped to do good to everyone" (2 Timothy 3:16,17, TLB).

A life of victory, power, joy, and fruitfulness will be experienced by any believer who studies the Bible and accepts it as God's infallible and holy Word to man. It tells us how to enjoy an intimate relationship with our heavenly Father and how to receive wisdom, love, and grace from Him.

If questions arise in your mind about the authority or accuracy of the Bible, do not hesitate to share them with other believers who can help you find answers. Or read books on the subject such as *Evidence That Demands a Verdict* by Josh McDowell or *The New Testament Documents: Are They Reliable?* by F. F. Bruce. I urge you not to allow your confidence in the integrity of the Bible to be diluted to the point where irreparable damage is done to your life and faith.

The Bible is God's personal love letter to His children.

The story is told of a young woman who heard about a popular novel. Intrigued, she began to read it but found it difficult to understand. She would read for a while, then put it down, then pick it up again whenever one of her friends told her how much she was enjoying it. But no matter how she tried to immerse herself in the book, it just did not hold her interest.

Then one day she met the author. Eventually, she fell in love with him. Now she could hardly wait to read his novel. This time, she found it to be the most captivating and exciting book she had ever read.

Before I became a Christian, I had difficulty reading the Bible. In fact, I found it boring. Then I experienced the love of its Author, the Lord Jesus Christ, and my attitude changed. I began to realize that the Bible is God's personal love letter to His children. I became excited about what He had to say to me.

Do you find the Bible the most interesting book in your library? Or are you tempted to read anything but the Bible? The best way to catch the excitement about reading God's Word is to experience and share the love of its Author.

The Bible reveals the character of God.

All throughout school, while on the faculty of a major university, and as a businessman in Hollywood, I was an agnostic. As a materialist and a humanist, I was dedicated to my own plans and purpose for life. The Bible was an unknown book to me.

Then through a series of wonderful circumstances, I began to learn about God and how He has revealed Himself to hundreds of millions through His only Son, Jesus Christ. I discovered that, according to the Scriptures, God the Son created the entire universe and holds everything together by the word of His command.

As I began to study the Bible, I found a true record of who God is and what He is like. His marvelous attributes filled me with wonder, reverence, and awe. Through the stories of how He led Old and New Testament believers, I saw proof of His love, wisdom, power, sovereignty, and holiness. More than fifty years later, I continue to grow in my love for Him as I am still discovering more about who God is.

I encourage you to make it your number one priority to get to know God—and to love Him with all your heart, soul, and mind (Matthew 22:37,38). Get to know what He thinks and how He acts. Knowing God intimately will change your life. When we read His Word and learn how much God loves and cares for us, we can trust Him with everything— our families, our possessions, and even with our own lives.

The Bible gives the most reasonable explanation of creation and the origin of mankind.

The Bible has the perfect explanation for the beginnings of all creation—an intelligent, powerful God who created everything with order and purpose (Genesis 1:1). Only a Being with supernatural power and unlimited ability could have fashioned something as intricate as a DNA molecule and as colossal as the Milky Way Galaxy. In fact, astronomers now believe that there are 100 billion galaxies. The Bible assures us that our great God and Savior created it all.

The Bible explains the reason for human suffering and evil behavior.

Have you ever wondered: *Why is there so much human suffering? Why is there war and poverty?* Many people blame God for these evils. But man, because he is self-centered and seeks his own way, creates wars and inhumanities. Sickness, death, earthquakes, tornadoes, and floods are part of God's judgment for mankind's sin.

Romans 5:12 explains, "When Adam sinned, sin entered the entire human race. His sin spread death throughout all the world, so everything began to grow old and die, for all sinned" (TLB). What better explanation have you heard for the mess our world is in? Biblical truth about man's evil nature is the only logical answer for cruelty, selfishness, pride, violence, disease, war, and death.

Former President Ronald Reagan stated that if all Americans would "live closer to the Commandments and the Golden Rule," the problems we face as individuals and as a nation would be solved.[4] I believe that this statement is true because only God—who understands the depravity of the human heart—has the answers to our sinfulness.

---

[4] Ronald Reagan, *Gales Quotations* CD-ROM (Detroit, MI: Gale Research Inc., 1995).

For this reason, I memorized both the Ten Commandments (found in Exodus 20) and the Golden Rule (found in Matthew 7:12) many years ago. I recite them every morning and evening to help me remember God's standards and to help me resist temptation when it arises.

The Bible contains the story of our Savior.

Of course, as humans we cannot live good enough lives on our own to achieve God's holy standards in the Ten Commandments or the Golden Rule. That comes through our faith in Jesus Christ and His Spirit living in us. The Bible is our source for understanding this truth.

One of the most convincing arguments for the authority and accuracy of Scripture is the fulfillment of Old Testament prophecies in the life of Jesus. Like a golden thread running from Genesis to Malachi, we find more than three hundred references to the Messiah. They are all fulfilled in the person of our Lord Jesus Christ.

Abraham Lincoln said, "I believe the Bible is the best gift God has given to man. All the good Savior gave to the world was communicated through this Book."[5] How true! The more we study the Bible, the better we will understand who Jesus is and what He has done for us. How thrilling to open its pages and find the love of God so clearly demonstrated through the life, teachings, death, and resurrection of His Son, Jesus Christ.

A study of God's Word contributes to Christian growth.

The Word of God is our fuel, our food for growth in the Christian faith. When we feed on its richness, we grow strong and healthy in our spiritual lives. Psalm 1 says:

---

[5] Abraham Lincoln, September 5, 1864, in an address to the Committee of Colored People from Baltimore.

> *Oh, the joys of those who do not follow evil men's advice, who do not hang around with sinners, scoffing at the things of God: But they delight in doing everything God wants them to, and day and night are always meditating on His laws and thinking about ways to follow Him more closely. They are like trees along a river bank bearing luscious fruit each season without fail. Their leaves shall never wither, and all they do shall prosper* (Psalm 1:1–3, TLB).

Unless the Bible becomes the basis of our faith, we will be swayed by our experiences, which can be dangerous. Do not misunderstand me. There is nothing wrong with experiences, emotions, and dreams—if they are validated by Scripture. But beware of depending only on experiences to build your faith. The Word of God is our one sure foundation. Obeying God's Word gives us assurance that what we are doing is right in God's eyes.

Obedience to the teaching and commands of the Bible results in joy and victory.

A believer cannot walk in the fullness and power of the Holy Spirit and radiate the love of Christ unless he is spending time in God's Word. But if he faithfully studies the Bible daily, he will avoid the emotional and spiritual problems that many believers experience and consider inevitable.

The Christian life is not without trials. While some are caused by events we cannot control, most are a result of disobedience to God's commands. The Christian who saturates his mind with God's Word will want to please the Lord in every way. God's Word will show him how to deal with temptation so he does not reap the consequences of wrongdoing.

When we read and obey God's Word, we learn how to live above our circumstances. We find the answers to the deep questions of life. As a result, we will live a life of incredible joy and victory!

The Bible contributes to a more vital witness for Christ.

The greatest spiritual harvest of all time is taking place today. More people are hearing the gospel, receiving Christ as their Savior, and committing themselves to helping fulfill the Great Commission than at any other time in history. How is this revolution taking place? Through the distribution and teaching of God's Word by faithful Christians who want to share their joy and victory in Christ with others.

Spending time daily with God in His Word gives us the power and excitement to spread His message of love and forgiveness. Studying the Bible helps us see how God loves the unlovable and seeks the lonely and hurting. Applying God's commands helps us maintain a godly life that demonstrates the Lord's presence in our lives to others.

A Commitment to Study the Bible

*M*ost believers will admit that knowing God's Word is important. The problem arises when we acknowledge the central place God's Word should have in our lives but do not change our lifestyle to reflect that fact.

The psalmist says in Psalm 119:4–8, "You have charged us to keep your commandments carefully. Oh, that my actions would consistently reflect your principles! Then I will not be disgraced when I compare my life with your commands. When I learn your righteous laws, I will thank you by living as I should!" "Living as I should" means having an attitude of expectancy and a desire for righteousness as we open God's Word. It also means determining ahead of time that we will make Bible reading and study a priority in our life.

For many years, I have had an incredibly full schedule of travel, with approximately three hundred days a year away from my home and office for meetings and speaking engagements. It would be easy for me to say, "I have so many commitments today that I just don't have time to spend with God in prayer and reading His Word." Yet if I miss that time alone with my Savior and Lord, I miss the best part of my day and do not accomplish all that God wants me to do in the remaining hours.

I can joyfully testify to the fact that when I give priority to reading, studying, and memorizing God's Word, the results are blessing without measure. The Holy Spirit illumines my mind and enables me to apply His wisdom to my heart. Time after time, moment by moment, my life has been enriched because I read, studied, and hid God's Word in my heart.

Just as God's Word made a lifelong difference in my life, it will do the same for yours. Right now, ask the Lord to give you a deep desire to study and understand His Word. Ask Him to help you apply what you learn to your daily living. Ask the Holy Spirit to teach you what you need to know (John 14:26). Make your prayer specific and practical.

Psalm 25:14 promises: "Friendship with the Lord is reserved for those who fear Him. With them He shares the secrets of His covenant." I assure you that as you read and study His Word with a fresh commitment, you will find a new intimacy with God and more joy than you have ever experienced before.

A Well-Rounded Plan for Knowing the Bible

*G*etting to know God's Word involves a plan for digging into God's message to you. When you personally received Christ as your Savior and Lord, you began a great adventure. That great adventure is mapped out for you in the pages of God's Word. To keep moving along the path of righteousness and walking with God in a fast-track world, we need to plan for a daily time with Him, reading His Word, memorizing Scripture, and studying the Bible in depth.

Build a plan for reading, memorizing, and studying the Bible into your schedule. Be flexible. Listen for the Holy Spirit's prompting about your pace and method. Do not become discouraged if you fail to make your appointment with God one day. Good habits take work to develop. Ask God to give you the motivation to stay on course. Let me give you a few guidelines on how to proceed in each area.

Set aside at least 15 minutes a day for a quiet time with our Lord.

The purpose of a quiet time is to enjoy the Lord and communicate with Him about every detail of your day. As we read a portion of Scripture and pray each day, we allow Him to speak to us in a personal way.

Some believers like to read through a small portion of Scripture and meditate on it. Others like to use daily devotional helps. These usually have a short Bible passage and a brief reading to go along with the passage. Your local Christian bookstore contains a wide variety of devotional books, including ones specifically written for men, women, youth, or couples. I recommend a book I wrote about the promises God has given us in His Word, called *Promises: A Daily Guide to Supernatural Living*. (See the resource list at the back of this book for ordering information.)

Use a notebook to record insights from God's Word, your prayer requests, praises to God, and thanks for answered prayer. For the last few minutes, just listen to God. Ask Him to speak to you through His Word. Think about what you have read and thank Him for what He has done for you.

Plan for about 15 minutes a day to read through the Bible in a year.

One of the most important things a Christian can do to grow in Christ, walk in the Spirit, and be a fruitful witness is to read the Bible through every year. I recommend reading it from cover to cover. For many years I have read the entire Bible during a 12-month period. This has been one of the richest blessings of my life.

John Stott, a great missionary statesman, recommends reading three chapters each day and studying one in depth. With this plan, you will complete the Bible in a year. But take into account that some chapters are much longer than others, so the time you spend each day will vary.

My mentor, the great Bible teacher Henrietta Mears, advocated a simple plan that is as relevant today as it was in her day. "Do you want to read the Bible through?" she asked. "Leave 80 hours for it. Plot out that time. How much time can you give each day? How many days a week? This is a highly practical proposition…We are all busy and must arrange for it."

In your local Christian bookstore, you will find Bible schedules to read through the Bible in one year. The advantage of using these plans is that they are marked by date. Many include daily readings from the Old Testament, New Testament, Psalms, and Proverbs. As you read, jot down any questions or meaningful passages so that you can return to them at a later time.

Take a few minutes each day to memorize Scripture.

Whenever many adults hear the word "memorize," they groan, "I could never do that." Yet all of us memorize many things in our daily lives: telephone numbers, account numbers, addresses, television commercial jingles, sayings by famous people. You have much more capacity to memorize than you realize.

We should memorize Scripture if for no other reason than the Lord commanded us to learn His Word (Proverbs 7:1–3). You will soon notice other changes in your life because the Holy Spirit will use the verses you learn to teach you new things and to help you resist temptation (Psalm 119:11). As a new believer, I memorized many verses. First Corinthians 10:13 alone has saved me from disobeying God on hundreds if not thousands of occasions. As we memorize God's Word, the verses become part of the inner workings of our mind and the Holy Spirit uses them to guide us through situations we encounter during our day.

Effective Scripture memory will just take a few minutes out of your day if you develop a systematic method. Then look for small slots of time that you normally waste and fill them with memorizing God's Word. For example, instead of reading a magazine in the doctor's office, memorize a verse of Scripture. Use your break at work or arrange to memorize Scripture with a fellow believer in your workplace, campus, or church. Memorize Scripture as a family.

I suggest you start by learning the verses in the *Four Spiritual Laws* and in the booklet *Have You Made the Wonderful Discovery of the Spirit-Filled Life?* (See the Resources at the back of this book.) These Bible verses will come in handy when you are sharing your faith in Christ and helping believers appropriate the power of the Holy Spirit. You can also find many good systems for memorization in your Christian bookstore. The Navigators are well-known for their wonderful Scripture memory resources.

Review is just as important as the initial memory stage. Here are some suggestions for organizing your review.

- Write your memory verses on 3×5-inch index cards and carry them with you to review whenever you have a few free moments.

- Use a pocket-sized notebook to write your verses and the dates on which you learned them. Review your list often.

- Build a chart of key verses that God has used in your life. Review them as you thank Him for how He has worked in your life.

- Keep a list of key verses from your personal or small-group Bible study which you memorized to make your study more meaningful. Review them periodically.

Dedicate a few hours each week for Bible study.

I encourage you to take personal responsibility to study the Bible. Plan a specific time and place in which to work on these studies. My wife, Vonette, and I begin every day on our knees in prayer together, usually just for five minutes. Then we separate and I study the Word of God on my knees as she studies too. We both want to spend that special time with our wonderful Savior.

If necessary, begin with five minutes a day and add more time as you go. Decide how and where you are going to do it. Most people find that a quiet corner in their home designated for Bible study enables them to draw away on a regular basis. You may find it more productive to work at a desk or table. If you already use the computer for other tasks, you may prefer keeping your files and notes on it. Usually, you will want to study the Bible on your own, working through a particular book of the Bible or examining the life of a Bible character. Other times, God may lead you to study with a friend or join a small-group study.

Before you begin your Bible study, you may want to obtain a few study aids. The following are basic tools: at least two different versions of the Bible; one topical study Bible; a concordance; a Bible dictionary; and books, workbooks, and tapes on the topic you chose to study. As you use your Bible study aids, remember that Bible study involves just that— studying the *Bible!* Do not allow yourself to rely so heavily on Bible study aids that God cannot teach you from His Word.

At this point you may be wondering, *How can I do all these Bible activities with my busy schedule?* How you balance these four ways of relating to God's Word will depend on your situation and your spiritual needs at the moment. Some days you may just have to make small adjustments in your daily routine to saturate yourself with God's Word. For example, at times I take a few moments to read the Bible like a love letter from God. During my prayer times, I pray through certain portions of Scripture. Vonette and I also play recordings of Scripture as we travel in the car or while we work at home. Other days, you may have to write time for God's Word into your schedule like any other priority appointments you may have.

An Overview of the Bible

*M*any people find it a bit intimidating to open the Bible, let alone try to study it. Yet what do you do when you first get a new book? Maybe you flip through it or glance at the Contents page. Why not approach Bible study the same way? Let me give you an overview of the parts of the Bible to make your study more meaningful.

The Bible is composed of two main sections: the Old Testament (containing 39 books) and the New Testament (containing 27 books). The Old Testament can be divided into four parts:

1. *Pentateuch* (5 books: Genesis, Exodus, Leviticus, Numbers, Deuteronomy). These five historical books, written by Moses, are called the books of the Law. They provide the basis for the promises and commandments God gave His people Israel.

2. *Historical* (12 books: Joshua, Judges, Ruth, 1 and 2 Samuel, 1 and 2 Kings, 1 and 2 Chronicles, Ezra, Nehemiah, Esther). These books tell of the establishment of the nation of Israel in the Promised Land, of Israel's repeated turning from God to sin, and finally of the Assyrian and Babylonian exile as God's punishment.

3. *Poetical* (5 books: Job, Psalms, Proverbs, Ecclesiates, Song of Solomon). The poetical books recount the human

experiences of the people of God in various aspects of earthly life.

4. *Prophetic* (17 books: Isaiah, Jeremiah, Lamentations, Ezekiel, and Daniel—the Major Prophets; Hosea, Joel, Amos, Obadiah, Jonah, Micah, Nahum, Habakkuk, Zephaniah, Haggai, Zechariah, and Malachi—the Minor Prophets). God raised up prophets in times of apostasy. They spoke on behalf of God to the heart and conscience of the nation of Israel. The prophetic messages have a twofold application: 1) local prophecies for the prophet's time, and 2) prophecies telling of God's divine purpose for the future, especially the coming of the Messiah.

The New Testament begins with the birth of Jesus and covers the history and teaching of the early Church. The New Testament can be divided into five parts:

1. *Gospels* (4 books: Matthew, Mark, Luke, John). These books record the eternal being, human ancestry, birth, teachings, death, resurrection, and ascension of Jesus Christ, the Son of God and Son of Man.

2. *The Acts of the Apostles* (1 book: Acts). In this book, God makes clear to man how His work is to be carried out in the power of the Holy Spirit. Acts also includes the history of the early Church.

3. *The Letters of Paul* (14 books: Romans, 1 and 2 Corinthians, Galatians, Ephesians, Philippians, Colossians, 1 and 2 Thessalonians, 1 and 2 Timothy, Titus, Philemon, Hebrews). Paul's letters answer troublesome questions that arose in the newly planted churches. Although he wrote to specific churches, he was representing the basic doctrines and teachings of Christ to the whole Christian world for centuries to come.

4. *General Epistles* (7 books: James; 1 and 2 Peter; 1, 2, and 3 John; Jude). These books were called General Epistles as early as the fourth century to distinguish them from the Epistles of Paul. (Epistle means letter.) Written by several authors, they were addressed to the Church in general.

5. *Prophecy* (1 book: Revelation). This book points to the final triumph of Jesus Christ as the culmination of God's plan for mankind. The book describes the close of the age and the coming glory of God. The writer portrays the Great Tribulation, the second coming of Christ, the doom of those who reject Him, and the ultimate reward for those who receive Him. Revelation also provides a glimpse of heaven and eternity with God.

A Basic Framework for In-Depth Bible Study

*B*ible study can be compared to taking an extended road trip. If you travel by automobile across the country, you need to develop driving skills and habits that will bring you safely to your destination. Some of these skills you probably do automatically, such as fastening your seat belt or adjusting your mirrors. Others, such as making sure your vehicle is in good shape, may require more planning and thought. While you drive, you also use certain skills, such as glancing in your rearview mirror and following road signs.

We also need to adopt good habits and skills in Bible study. I suggest the following patterns as part of your Bible study regimen. Some may require effort on your part; others may be easy to implement.

- Begin with *prayer*. Ask the Holy Spirit to give you an understanding of God's Word and the power to apply its principles to your everyday life.
- Keep a *Bible study notebook* at your desk or on your laptop —and use it!
- *Read the text slowly* and carefully, then reread and take notes.
- End your time in *prayer*, thanking God for what you have learned.
- *Obey* the commands and follow the instructions you learn

from God's Word. Strive to be a doer of the Word and not just a hearer (James 1:22–25) through the power of the Holy Spirit. No matter how much you know about God's Word, if you do not apply what you learn, you will be wasting your time.

An extended road trip also requires a good map. Many travelers like to highlight all the highways they will take so they can glance at the map at any time to ensure they are on course.

I want to share two "maps" or plans for your study. Each is simple to use and to remember. I will give the basic thrust of the plans, then show you how to use them in the sample projects in the practice section of this book. The first plan uses the following four points (note the italicized words):

1. What does the passage *say?*
   With this question, determine simple facts such as who the passage is talking about, the general subject and subtopics, and the setting. Also look for basic information such as when the event occurred (historical and cultural background) and the characteristics of the main character.

2. What does the passage *mean?*
   From the basic facts, you can then find the meaning in the text. Identify the main principles and the lessons learned. To help you understand areas that are not clear to you in the passage, look up cross-references before you consult your study aids. Remember that the Bible is its own best commentary.

3. How can I *apply* the passage to my daily life?
   Design an action plan to put the principles and lessons into practice. Then write out a personal prayer related to the main application asking the Holy Spirit to help you apply it to your life.

4. How does this passage *fit* into or relate to the rest of Scripture?

No passage of Scripture stands alone. Each correlates with the whole theme of a chapter, book, and the entire Bible. Read other portions of Scripture related to the passage you are studying to see how they fit together. Also scan the entire book in which the passage is recorded to get a clearer idea of how the passage relates to the whole.

To make this study plan easier, just remember four key words: Say, Mean, Apply, Fit.

Here is another simple plan you can use. I call it the "4 Ts." They are:

1. *Then:* Write down what the passage meant to the people for whom it was written.

2. *Timeless:* Look for principles that transcend the period in which the passage was written.

3. *Today:* Apply the timeless truth to today's world.

4. *To Me:* Then apply the timeless principle to a specific area in your life.

Let us say for the sake of our road-trip analogy that we plan to explore four different states on our trip. We will want to stop at a number of interesting sites in each state. Before we leave, we will plan these stops with the under-standing that we can make unexpected detours at other fas-cinating places as we go.

In our Bible study, we also have four "states," or methods, we can explore. They are: book study, chapter study, topical study, and biographical study. Each will give us unique and fascinating insights into what God has written to us.

In the following practice sections, I have selected one of the two plans (or maps) for each of the four methods (or states). The plan is shown in bold type. The instructions accompanying each point will help stimulate your thinking. I encourage you to use these questions and instructions until you feel confident in applying the method on your own. Then adapt the plans to fit your needs. As in a road trip, as you journey through your study, be prepared to find things you are not expecting as God reveals His truth to you.

BOOK STUDY: 1 John

I recommend starting with 1 John, a short book that closely follows the more familiar Gospel of John. For this study, we will work through the Say, Mean, Apply, and Fit plan.

What does it *say*?

- Read through the book.
- Reread the book. Mark and underline content as God speaks to you.
- Select a key verse for the entire book, then memorize it.
- List the principal characters and their significance.
- From each chapter, select key verses to memorize.

What does it *mean*?

- Outline the book in your own words, noting themes.
- Notice what is repeated in the text. These are main principles for us to learn.
- Write down principles from the lives of the main characters.
- Refer to a good commentary or Study Bible to find additional insights.

How can I *apply* it?

- List teachings to obey and promises to claim.
- Write down ways to apply what you have learned.
- Meditate on the attributes of God the Father, Son, and Holy Spirit.
- Pray by using words from this passage to express your thoughts.

How does it *fit*?

- Using cross-references, look up other passages on the main topics covered in the book.

- For your ongoing study, set up a folder for each book of the Bible. Slip in sermon notes, articles, or other material that will help you in your study. Also include the study notes you write as you work through the book. On the cover of the folder, list the dates you did your study.
- As you complete each new book, compare the themes, promises, and commands with those of other books you have studied.

CHAPTER STUDY: Psalm 119

Almost all of the 176 verses in Psalm 119 address our need for the Word of God in everyday Christian living. A deeper look at this chapter will help you better understand the priority God places on knowing and obeying His Word. I have used the 4 Ts to organize this study.

Then:

- *Perspective:* What is the setting and background?
- *People:* Who are the principal characters? What problems did they encounter?

Timeless:

- *Preview:* What is the main focus of this chapter?
- *Principles:* What are the most important lessons to be learned? What do they teach about God the Father, Son, and Holy Spirit?
- *Priority:* What is the key verse? Memorize it.

Today:

- *Purpose for today:* How do the timeless truths apply to today's society?
- *Pattern:* How are the people and situations the same today as they were in Bible times?

To Me:

- *Promises:* Are there promises for me to claim?

- *Practical application:*

  Is there an example for me to follow?

  Is there sin for me to confess?

  Is there an attitude or a behavior for me to correct?

- *Prayer:* Is there a prayer for me to echo?

TOPICAL OR WORD STUDY: "God's Word"

For this study, you will need a topical study Bible and concordance. Identify a key word or phrase, like "God's Word" or "love" or "the Holy Spirit." As you accumulate material, divide the topic into subgroups. Subgroups vary, but usually fall into additional word or topic categories. (Note that you will not find the word *Bible* in the Bible; it comes from the Greek word *biblos*.)

Say:

- *Word subgroups:* Many different translations of Hebrew and Greek words refer to God's Word. Make a list of them, including the references where they are found.

- Quickly read through the Scriptures you have noted and jot down the main facts in the verses.

- *Topic subgroups:* For practice, look at "God's Word and the Trinity." Research passages where a member of the Trinity affirms the truth of the living Word.

Mean:

- How does the eternal nature of God's Word affect us?

- What is God revealing to me through this study?

Apply:

- What adjustments do I need to make in my attitudes and actions?

- Write a prayer of response to God.

Fit:

- How do the terms for God's Word differ between the Old Testament and the New Testament?
- How do the principles about God's Word complement each other between the two Testaments?

BIOGRAPHICAL STUDY: Timothy

Did you know that there are 2,930 people mentioned in the Bible? Studying an individual's life is often very enlightening. You will need a topical study Bible or concordance for this study. If you plan to use a Bible dictionary, delay reading it until you have finished your own thorough research of texts mentioning the person you want to study. Organize the material you uncover into an outline. Or try another creative expression of what you learn—compose a song, write a poem, sketch the character, write a short story. For this study, we will apply the 4 Ts to the life of Timothy.

Then:

- *Background:*

  What was the social and political atmosphere in which he lived?

  How did this impact his life?

  What do we know of his family?

  What kind of training did he have?

- *Major life experiences:*

  What did he accomplish during his lifetime?

  Did he experience a great crisis? How did he face it?

- *Character sketch:*

  What are his outstanding personality traits?

  Who were his friends? What kind of people were they?

  Do you see any signs of character growth and development?

  Are particular strengths and weaknesses evident?

  Who influenced him? Who did he influence?

- *Spiritual life:*
  What was his experience with God?
  Was there any outstanding sin in his life?
  What was its nature and effect on his future life?

Timeless:

- What is similar between the problems faced by the Bible character and the problems we face today?
- What are the lessons to be learned?
- What biblical principles did he use to grow to spiritual maturity?

Today:

- What solutions applied by the Bible character still work today?
- What steps to joy and victory are still effective today?

To Me:

- Was there some lesson in this person's life that touched me?
- What can I learn from this person's life that will help me in my walk with God?

Everyone needs a balanced diet for good spiritual nourishment. You will probably want to vary your methods between book, chapter, topical, and biographical to meet different needs and to keep your study of God's Word fresh and exciting.

I encourage you to persevere in your Bible study even when it becomes difficult. In a road trip, some stretches of highway will be difficult to travel. You may have to climb mountains or navigate through rainstorms. Other times you will get weary. But those times will fade in the joy of discovering something you have never before seen or experienced from the eternal realm of our God. I assure you that the trip through God's Word will be more thrilling than any challenge you have ever undertaken!

Our Richest Treasure

Truly, the Bible is our richest treasure. We must not take it for granted. A few years ago when the former Soviet Union opened up to the gospel as the communist government collapsed, I met with one of the most influential generals in the Russian military. I had the incredible joy of giving him a Bible.

He took the book with a sense of awe. He said slowly, "I have never had a Bible before. This is the first Bible I have ever held in my hand." Can you imagine this commanding general, in the prime of his career, staring in wonder as he actually held God's Word in his hands?

I encourage you to have that same awe and wonder as you begin your adventure in God's Word. It will become a part of your life and will guide you as you open its pages and drink deeply of its wisdom.

I have read and studied the Bible since 1945 when I received Christ as my Lord and Savior. While running my personal businesses, I completed five years of graduate work at Princeton Theological Seminary and Fuller Theological Seminary. After all these years of reading, studying, and memorizing God's Word, it is still by far the most exciting and wonderful book in my library of thousands of volumes.

Keep one essential principle in mind as you saturate yourself in the Bible—the Holy Spirit is the key to opening the treasure box of God's Word. Jesus promised His followers a full and abundant life, but it is impossible to know and experience that wonderful life of the Spirit without a familiar understanding of God's Word. I like to explain the principle like this. The wings of an airplane represent the life of the believer. One wing represents the Person and ministry of the Holy Spirit. The other wing represents the Word of God. Just as a plane cannot fly without both wings, neither can a believer in Christ really "fly" apart from hiding the Word of

God in his heart and being filled, controlled, and empowered by the Holy Spirit.

Therefore, the key to effective Bible study is to ask the Holy Spirit to teach us the Word as we study. I urge you to make the following prayer your own as you begin your journey through God's Word:

Father in heaven, I know that the Bible is Your holy, inspired love letter to man. I realize that I cannot know You and Your plan for my life apart from the truths contained in Your Word. I want to read, study, memorize, and meditate on Your Word daily as a way of life, but I need the inspiration of the Holy Spirit to help me.

Through the enabling of the Holy Spirit, I commit time daily to discover the treasure of Your Word so that I can love and serve You to my maximum ability for the honor, glory, worship, and praise of Your holy and majestic name as the Father, Son, and Holy Spirit. Amen.

With this key to unlock the treasure, begin the journey of your life!

NOTE

Remember, *How You Can Study the Bible Effectively* is a transferable concept. You can master it by reading it six times; then pass it on to others as our Lord commands us in Matthew 28:20, "Teach these new disciples to obey all the commands I have given you" (TLB). The apostle Paul encourages us to do the same: "The things you have heard me say in the presence of many witnesses entrust to reliable men who will also be qualified to teach others" (2 Timothy 2:2).

Self-Study Guide

1. Make a list of ways God's Word has benefited your life. Begin with the fact that it contains the message of God's love and forgiveness which introduced you to eternal life in Christ. When you complete your list, thank God for each item.

2. Now list and thank God for the benefits of His Word as found in the following verses in Psalm 119:

   2,3: happy
   9: pure
   11: heart, not sin
   25: revive
   28: strengthen me
   45: walk at liberty
   49,50: hope, comfort, life
   52: take comfort
   61: do not forget your law
   130: your words give light
   133: steady, promise
   143: commandments are my delight
   144: understanding that I may live
   163: I love your law!

3. Compare your two lists from questions 1 and 2. What did you find in Psalm 119 that you would like to add to your personal list?

4. Of the nine reasons why the Bible is the most important book (pages 9–16), which one means the most to you right now? Why?

5. For each of the following statements, circle the reponse that is most accurate:

   • I have a daily quiet time:

a. Every day   c. Once in a while
b. Almost every day   d. Rarely

- I study the Bible:
  a. Every day   c. A few times a year
  b. Every week   d. Only in my church's Bible study

- I have read through the Bible:
  a. Many times   c. I got started but never completed it
  b. Once   d. I have never attempted it

- I memorize Scripture:
  a. Regularly   c. Only when I was a child
  b. Once in a while   d. I didn't know it was important

6. Evaluate your responses to question 5. Which areas do you need to concentrate on? Which area will you work on first? Write a plan for implementing this area into your schedule. (When you are successful with this area, go on to the others until you are successful in all areas.)

7. What is the Holy Spirit's role in Bible Study? (See John 14:26.)

8. What is the role of God's Word in Bible study? (See Hebrews 4:12,13.)

9. How do these two roles work together in a believer's life?

10. Select one of the Bible study methods given on pages 25–26 and work through it. Then answer these questions:

- What was hard about completing the study? How can I work on those areas?

- What insights from the study are most important to me right now?

Group Discussion Questions

1. Skim through Psalm 119. What are some of the benefits of God's Word found in this chapter?

2. How has God used His Word in your life to accomplish His purposes?

3. In what ways do you feel the Bible is a love letter to you?

4. Hebrews 4:12,13 describes how God's Word works in helping us live righteously.

   - How does it make you feel when you realize that God knows everything about you?

   - What security does that knowledge give you?

5. Psalm 1:1–3 says that God's Word contributes to our spiritual growth. In what ways has this happened in your life?

6. In what ways can the following activities in God's Word build your faith in God?

   - Having a quiet time
   - Reading through the Bible
   - Memorizing Scripture
   - In-depth Bible study

7. What practical steps have you already taken to incorporate one of these activities into your schedule?

8. What practical steps will you take to incorporate the activities you do not now practice into your daily schedule? Be specific.

9. What is the Holy Spirit's role in Bible study? (See John 14:26.)

Fasting & Prayer

In 1994, I felt led by God to undergo a 40-day fast. During that time, God impressed on me that He was going to send a great spiritual awakening to America, and that this revival would be preceded by a time of spiritual preparation through repentance, with a special emphasis on fasting and prayer. In 2 Chronicles 7:14, God gives us a promise of hope that involves repentance:

If my people, who are called by my name, will humble themselves and pray and seek my face and turn from their wicked ways, then will I hear from heaven and will forgive their sin and will heal their land.

Fasting is the only spiritual discipline that meets all the conditions of 2 Chronicles 7:14. When a person fasts, he humbles himself; he has more time to pray; he has more time to seek God's face, and certainly he would turn from all known sin. One could read the Bible, pray, or witness for Christ without repenting of his sins. But one cannot enter into a genuine fast with a pure heart and pure motive and not meet the conditions of this passage.

Because of this promise, God has led me to pray that at least two million North Americans will fast and pray for forty days for an awakening in America and the fulfillment of the Great Commission. As millions of Christians rediscover the power of fasting as it relates to the holy life, prayer, and witnessing, they will come alive. Out of this great move of God's Spirit will come the revival for which we have all prayed so long, resulting in the fulfillment of the Great Commission.

I invite you to become one of the two million who will fast and pray for forty days. Also, I encourage you to attend the Fasting & Prayer gatherings held each year. If you feel God leading you to participate, please let us know on the Response Form. For more information, see the Resources or call (800) 888-FAST.

Other Resources by Bill Bright

Resources for Fasting and Prayer

The Coming Revival: America's Call to Fast, Pray, and "Seek God's Face." This inspiring yet honest book explains how the power of fasting and prayer by millions of God's people can usher in a mighty spiritual revival and lift His judgment on America. *The Coming Revival* can equip Christians, their churches, and our nation for the greatest spiritual awakening since the first century.

7 Basic Steps to Successful Fasting and Prayer. This handy booklet gives practical steps to undertaking and completing a fast, suggests a plan for prayer, and offers an easy-to-follow daily nutritional schedule.

Preparing for the Coming Revival: How to Lead a Successful Fasting and Prayer Gathering. In this easy-to-use handbook, the author presents step-by-step instructions on how to plan and conduct a fasting and prayer gathering in your church or community. The book also contains creative ideas for teaching group prayer and can be used for a small group or large gatherings.

The Transforming Power of Fasting and Prayer. This follow-up book to *The Coming Revival* includes stirring accounts of Christians who have participated in the fasting and prayer movement that is erupting across the country.

Five Steps to Fasting and Prayer. The need for Christians who can lead our nation out of its moral morass is desperate. Fasting and prayer can be the answer for those who desire a deeper walk with God—and to influence our society for Christ. This five-part study teaches you how to tap into the power of fasting and prayer.

Resources for Group and Individual Study

Five Steps of Christian Growth. This five-lesson Bible study will help group members be sure that they are a Christian, learn what it means to grow as a Christian, experience the joy of God's love and forgiveness, and discover how to be filled with the Holy Spirit. Leader's and Study Guides are available.

Five Steps to Sharing Your Faith. This Bible study is designed to help Christians develop a lifestyle of introducing others to Jesus Christ. With these step-by-step lessons, believers can learn how to share their faith with confidence through the power of the Holy Spirit. Leader's and Study Guides are available.

Five Steps to Knowing God's Will. This five-week Bible study will help you apply the Sound Mind Principle to discover God's will. Both new and more mature Christians will find clear instructions useful for every aspect of decision-making. Leader's and Study Guides are available.

Five Steps to Making Disciples. This effective Bible study can be used for one-on-one discipleship, leadership evangelism training in your church, or a neighborhood Bible study group. Participants will learn how to begin a Bible study to disciple new believers as well as more mature Christians. Leader's and Study Guides are available.

Ten Basic Steps Toward Christian Maturity. These time-tested Bible studies offer a simple way to understand the basics of the Christian faith and provide believers with a solid foundation for growth. The product of many years of extensive development, the studies have been used by thousands. Leader's and Study Guides are available.

Introduction: The Uniqueness of Jesus
Step 1: The Christian Adventure
Step 2: The Christian and the Abundant Life

Step 3: The Christian and the Holy Spirit
Step 4: The Christian and Prayer
Step 5: The Christian and the Bible
Step 6: The Christian and Obedience
Step 7: The Christian and Witnessing
Step 8: The Christian and Giving
Step 9: Exploring the Old Testament
Step 10: Exploring the New Testament

A Handbook for Christian Maturity. This book combines the *Ten Basic Steps* Study Guides in one handy volume. The lessons can be used for daily devotions or in groups of all sizes.

Ten Basic Steps Leader's Guide. This book contains teacher's helps for the entire *Ten Basic Steps* Bible Study series. The lessons include opening and closing prayers, objectives, discussion starters, and suggested answers to the questions.

Resources for Christian Growth

Transferable Concepts. This series of time-tested messages teaches the principles of abundant Christian life and ministry. These "back-to-the-basics" resources help Christians grow toward greater spiritual maturity and fulfillment and live victorious Christian lives. These messages, available in book format and on video or audio cassette, include:

How You Can Be Sure You Are a Christian
How You Can Experience God's Love and Forgiveness
How You Can Be Filled With the Spirit
How You Can Walk in the Spirit
How You Can Be a Fruitful Witness
How You Can Introduce Others to Christ
How You Can Help Fulfill the Great Commission
How You Can Love By Faith
How You Can Pray With Confidence
How You Can Experience the Adventure of Giving

A Man Without Equal. This book explores the unique birth, life, teachings, death, and resurrection of Jesus Christ and shows how He continues to change the way we live and think today. Available in book and video formats.

Life Without Equal. This inspiring book shows how Christians can experience pardon, purpose, peace, and power for living the Christian life. The book also explains how to release Christ's resurrection power to help change the world.

Have You Made the Wonderful Discovery of the Spirit-Filled Life? This booklet shows how you can discover the reality of the Spirit-filled life and live in moment-by-moment dependence on God.

The Holy Spirit: Key to Supernatural Living. This booklet helps you enter into the Spirit-filled life and explains how you can experience power and victory.

Promises: A Daily Guide to Supernatural Living. These 365 devotionals will help you remain focused on God's great love and faithfulness by reading and meditating on His promises each day. You will find your faith growing as you get to know our God and Savior better.

GOD: Discover His Character. Everything about our lives is determined and influenced by our view of God. Through these pages Dr. Bright will equip you with the biblical truths that will energize your walk with God. So when you're confused, you can experience His truth. When you're frightened, you can know His peace. When you're sad, you can live in His joy.

GOD: Discover His Character Video Series. In these 13 sessions, Dr. Bright's clear teaching is illustrated by fascinating dramas that bring home the truth of God's attributes in everyday life. This video series, with the accompanying leader's guide, is ideal for youth, college, and adult Sunday school classes or study groups.

Our Great Creator (Vol. 1). Dr. Bright explores God as all-powerful, ever-present, all-knowing, and sovereign—and how those attributes can give you hope and courage in life.

Our Perfect Judge (Vol. 2). God your perfect Judge, is holy, true, righteous, and just, and Dr. Bright explains how those characteristics help you to live a righteous life.

Our Gracious Savior (Vol. 3). Dr. Bright introduces you to the God who is loving, merciful, faithful, and unchangeable, and shows how you can experience those awesome attributes every day.

Resources for Evangelism

Witnessing Without Fear. This best-selling, Gold Medallion book offers simple hands-on, step-by-step coaching on how to share your faith with confidence. The chapters give specific answers to questions people most often encounter in witnessing and provide a proven method for sharing your faith.

Reaching Your World Through Witnessing Without Fear. This six-session video provides the resources needed to sensitively share the gospel effectively. Each session begins with a captivating dramatic vignette to help viewers apply the training. Available in individual study and group packages.

Have You Heard of the Four Spiritual Laws? This booklet is one of the most effective evangelistic tools ever developed. It presents a clear explanation of the gospel of Jesus Christ, which helps you open a conversation easily and share your faith with confidence.

Would You Like to Know God Personally? Based on the *Four Spiritual Laws*, this booklet uses a friendly, conversational format to present four principles for establishing a personal relationship with God.

Jesus and the Intellectual. Drawing from the works of notable scholars who affirm their faith in Jesus Christ, this booklet shows that Christianity is based on irrefutable historic facts. Good for sharing with unbelievers and new Christians.

A Great Adventure. Written as from one friend to another, this booklet explains how to know God personally and experience peace, joy, meaning, and fulfillment in life.

Sharing Christ Using the Four Spiritual Laws (audio cassette). Imagine being personally trained by Bill Bright to use the remarkable *Four Spiritual Laws* booklet. Through a five-part teaching series on *WorldChangers Radio*, this cassette will increase your confidence level and desire to share the good news with those you know.

Would You Like to Belong to God's Family? Designed for elementary-age young people, this booklet gives the simple message of salvation and includes the first steps for starting their new life in Christ. (Based on the *Four Spiritual Laws*.)

Resources by Vonette Bright

The Joy of Hospitality: Fun Ideas for Evangelistic Entertaining. Co-written with Barbara Ball, this practical book tells how to share your faith through hosting barbecues, coffees, holiday parties, and other events in your home.

The Joy of Hospitality Cookbook. Filled with uplifting Scriptures and quotations, this cookbook contains hundreds of delicious recipes, hospitality tips, sample menus, and family traditions that are sure to make your entertaining a memorable and eternal success. Co-written with Barbara Ball.

Beginning Your Journey of Joy. This adaptation of the *Four Spiritual Laws* speaks in the language of today's women and offers a slightly feminine approach to sharing God's love with your neighbors, friends, and family members.

These and other products from NewLife Publications are available from your favorite bookseller or by calling **(800) 235-7255** *(within U.S.) or* **(407) 826-2145** *(outside U.S.).*

BILL BRIGHT is founder and president of Campus Crusade for Christ International. Serving in 181 major countries representing 98 percent of the world's population, he and his dedicated team of more than 113,000 full-time staff, associate staff, and trained volunteers have introduced tens of millions of people to Jesus Christ, discipling millions to live Spirit-filled, fruitful lives of purpose and power for the glory of God.

Dr. Bright did graduate study at Princeton and Fuller Theological seminaries from 1946 to 1951. The recipient of many national and international awards, including five honorary doctorates, he is the author of numerous books and publications committed to helping fulfill the Great Commission. His special focus is *NewLife2000*, an international effort to help reach more than six billion people with the gospel of our Lord Jesus Christ by the year 2000.

Response Form

○ I have received Jesus Christ as my Savior and Lord as a result of reading this book.

○ I am a new Christian and want to know Christ better and experience the abundant Christian life.

○ With God's help I will faithfully pray for revival, the harvest, laborers, and donors.

○ I want to be one of the two million people who will join Dr. Bright in forty days of prayer and fasting for revival in America and the world, and the fulfillment of the Great Commission.

○ Please send me *free* information on opportunities with Campus Crusade for Christ: ○ full-time staff, ○ mid-career change, ○ part-time associate, ○ volunteer, ○ short-term trip, ○ summer intern, or ○ employment.

○ Please send me *free* information about other books, booklets, audiocassettes, videos, CDs, and other resources by Bill and Vonette Bright.

_____

NAME (please print)

_____

ADDRESS

_____

CITY   STATE   ZIP

_____

COUNTRY   E-MAIL

Please check the appropriate box(es), clip, and mail this form to:

> Dr. Bill Bright
> Campus Crusade for Christ
> P.O. Box 620877
> Orlando, FL 32862-0877 U.S.A.

You may also fax your response to (407) 826-2149, or send E-mail to newlifepubs@ccci.org. Visit our websites at www.newlifepubs.com, www.discovergod.com, and www.rsm.org.